Suzuki® Flute School
PIANO ACCOMPANIMENTS
VOLUME 6

by Toshio Takahashi

CONTENTS

Copyright © 1988 Dr. Shinichi Suzuki
Sole publisher for the entire world except Japan:
Summy-Birchard Inc.
exclusively distributed by
Warner Bros. Publications
15800 NW 48th Avenue
Miami, Florida 33014

ISBN 0-87487-382-7
3 5 7 9 11 13 15 14 12 10 8 6 4 2

INTRODUCTION

FOR THE STUDENT: This material is part of the worldwide Suzuki Method of teaching. Companion recordings should be used with these publications. In addition, there are flute part books that go along with this material.

FOR THE TEACHER: In order to be an effective Suzuki teacher, a great deal of ongoing education is required. Your national Suzuki association provides this for its membership. Teachers are encouraged to become members of their national Suzuki associations and maintain a teacher training schedule, in order to remain current, via institutes, short and long term programs. You are also encouraged to join the International Suzuki Association.

FOR THE PARENT: Credentials are essential for any teacher that you choose. We recommend you ask your teacher for his or her credentials, especially listing those relating to training in the Suzuki Method. The Suzuki Method experience should be a positive one, where there exists a wonderful, fostering relationship between child, parent and teacher. So choosing the right teacher is of the utmost importance.

In order to obtain more information about the Suzuki Method, please contact your country's Suzuki Association, the International Suzuki Association at 3-10-15 Fukashi, Matsumoto City 390, Japan, The Suzuki Association of the Americas, 1900 Folsom, #101, Boulder, Colorado 80302, or Summy-Birchard Inc., c/o Warner Bros. Publications, 15800 N.W. 48th Avenue, Miami, FL 33014, for current Associations' addresses.

1
Concerto For Two Flutes
1st Movement

D. Cimarosa

15

16

2
Suite No. 2 in B minor
1. Polonaise

J. S. BACH

Polonaise D.C.

2. Menuet

Allegretto (♩ = cca 100)

3. Badinerie

4. Ouverture

29

Lentement (Grave)